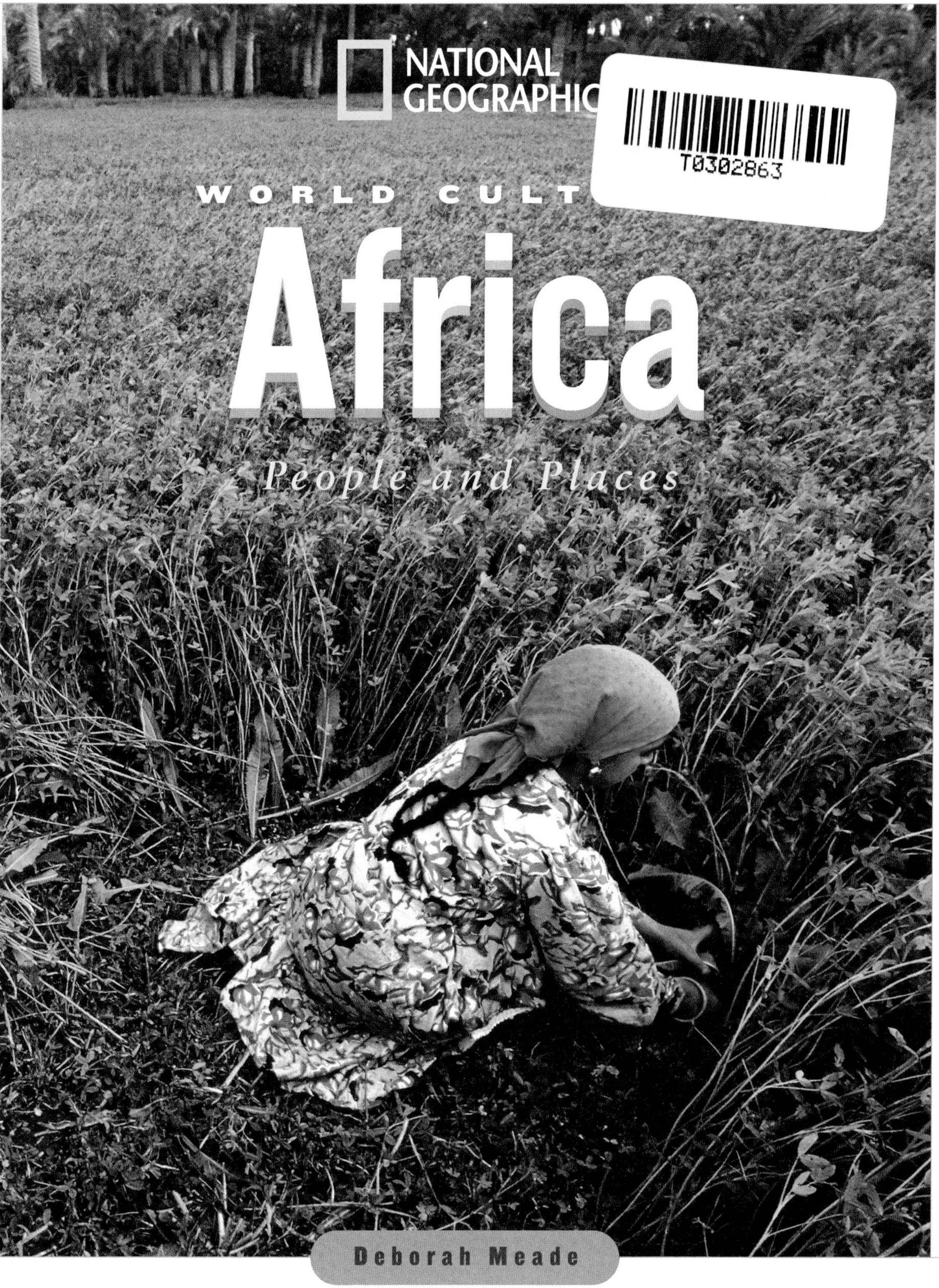

NATIONAL GEOGRAPHIC

WORLD CULT

Africa

People and Places

Deborah Meade

The British introduced soccer to Zanzibar in the 1930s, and the islanders took to it with a passion. Two boys, are seen here, practicing their skills.

PICTURE CREDITS

Cover (left), 2-3, 39, 56; Back Cover; Michael S. Lewis/NGIC; Cover (upper right), 14; Steve St. John; Cover (lower right),1,2-3; Kenneth Garrett/NGIC; 4(left), 12(lower), 59; David Turnley/Corbis; 4(right), 26-7, 28; Jerry Hardman-Jones/From Permanent Collection Chapungu Sculpture Park; 5(upper left), 5(lower left), 24, 32, 35, 47, 58; AFP/Corbis; 5 (upper right), 37, 38; Chenai Okammor; 5(lower right), 52-3, 59; Peter Turnley/Corbis; 8 (inset); John Kirkpatrick; 8-9; Peace Corps; 11 George Steinmetz; 12 up; Craig Aurness/Corbis; 13; Sue Matulaitis;; 16(upper); Attar Maher/Corbis; 16(lower), 63; George F. Mobley/NGIC; 17; Charles & Josette Lenars/Corbis; 18; Winfield Parks/NG; 19; Jodi Cobb; 20(left); Reuters/Ralph Orlowski; 20(right); Cambridge University Press; 22, 25; Reuters NewMedia Inc./Corbis; 23; Soul Buddyz;; 29, 49; James L. Stanfield/NGIC; 30, 30(inset), 31; Celia Winter Irving; 34; Brian J. Myers @ Photo Run; 40-1, 43; Carol Beckwith/Angela Fisher Robert Estall Photo Library; 42(upper); Roger De La Harpe; Gallo Images/Corbis; 42(lower); Adrian Arbib/Corbis; 44-5; Florence Wambugu/Modifying Africa; 46; Sarah Leen/NGIC; 48; Albert Moldvay/NG; 49(upper) Joseph H. Bailey/NG; 50; Campbell William/Corbis Sygma; 54; Steve McCurry; 55; Nubar Alexanian/Corbis; 60; Willis D. Vaughn

National Geographic Image Collection (NGIC); National Geographic (NG)

TEXT CREDITS

20-21, Chike and the River, © Cambridge University Press 1966. Reprinted with the permission of Cambridge University Press. 23; From Women's Enews, "South Africa Facing Loss of Its Teachers to AIDS," September 5, 2002.;34, From Pittsburgh Post-Gazette, "Fast Forward: Lornah and Her Camp for Girls," May 8, 2002; 35: From The Japan Times, "Departing Senegal the Pride of Africa," June 25, 2002.

Produced through the worldwide resources of the National Geographic Society, John M. Fahey, Jr., President and Chief Executive Officer; Gilbert M. Grosvenor, Chairman of the Board; Nina D. Hoffman, Executive Vice President and President, Books and Education Publishing Group.

PREPARED BY NATIONAL GEOGRAPHIC SCHOOL PUBLISHING

Ericka Markman, Senior Vice President and President, Children's Books and Education Publishing Group; Steve Mico, Vice President, Editorial Director; Richard Easby, Editorial Manager; Anne Pollard, Editor; Jim Hiscott, Design Manager; Kristin Hanneman, Illustrations Manager; Matt Wascavage, Manager of Publishing Services; Sean Philpotts, Production Manager; Jane Ponton, Production Artist.

MANUFACTURING AND QUALITY CONTROL

Christopher A. Liedel, Chief Financial Officer; Phillip L. Schlosser, Director; Clifton M. Brown, Manager.

CONSULTANTS/REVIEWERS

Martha Sharma, Geography Teacher, National Cathedral School, Washington, D.C.: Dr. Christine Drake, Professor of Geography, Old Dominion University

BOOK DEVELOPMENT

Summer Street Press, LLC

BOOK DESIGN

3R1 Group

PICTURE EDITING AND MANAGEMENT

National Geographic Image Sales: Lori Franklin, Picture Editor

MAP DEVELOPMENT AND PRODUCTION

National Geographic Map Division

Published by the National Geographic Society
1145 17th Street, N.W.
Washington, D.C. 20036-4688

ISBN: 0-7922-4365-X

Fifth Printing December, 2004
Printed in Canada

TABLE OF CONTENTS

What is Culture?

Culture is the way of life of a group of people. What languages do people speak? How do they worship? What kinds of traditions do they follow? How do they dress, eat, learn, and have fun? All of these are questions about culture.

Think about your own culture. Could you describe it easily? Probably not—cultures can be complicated and difficult to summarize. They also constantly change. Just as people grow and change over time, so too do their ways of life.

This book views culture from several different perspectives. As you read about the ways of life of some of Africa's people, think about how their cultures might compare to your own.

POPULATION

Population refers to people. It can mean the number of people who live in a place. It can also refer to how crowded or uncrowded a place is, what health conditions are present there, and how people in different places educate themselves.

ARTS

The way people use art to express themselves and decorate their surroundings is part of their culture. One very popular art form in Africa is sculpture.

SPORTS

Are sports an important part of the culture at your school? People around the world enjoy games and athletic activities.

TRADITIONS

Traditions are ways of doing things that one generation hands down to the next. A wedding ceremony is an important tradition in most of the world's cultures.

ECONOMY

The way a country uses resources to provide people with goods and services is called its economy. Farming, mining, and manufacturing help people to meet their basic needs and support their way of life.

GOVERNMENT

The purposes of a country's government include making laws, keeping order, preserving freedoms, and defending borders. People might wait in long lines to vote, or choose their leaders, because they wish to have control over how they are governed.

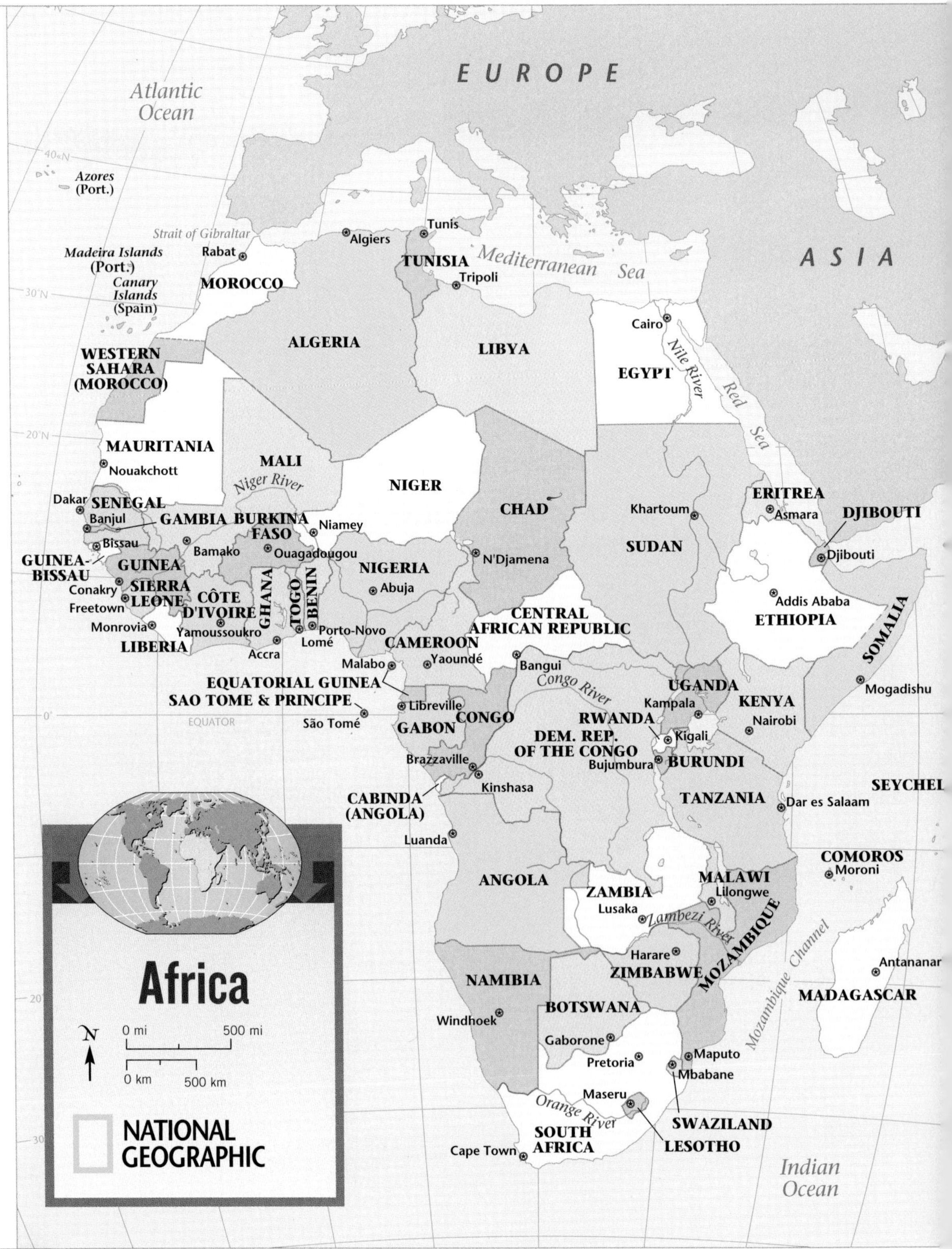

EUROPE
ASIA
Atlantic Ocean
Azores (Port.)
Strait of Gibraltar
Madeira Islands (Port.)
Canary Islands (Spain)
Mediterranean Sea
Rabat
Algiers
Tunis
TUNISIA
Tripoli
MOROCCO
ALGERIA
LIBYA
Cairo
EGYPT
Nile River
Red Sea
WESTERN SAHARA (MOROCCO)
MAURITANIA
Nouakchott
MALI
Niger River
NIGER
CHAD
SUDAN
Khartoum
ERITREA
Asmara
DJIBOUTI
Djibouti
Dakar
SENEGAL
Banjul
GAMBIA
BURKINA FASO
Niamey
Bissau
GUINEA-BISSAU
Bamako
Ouagadougou
GUINEA
NIGERIA
N'Djamena
Conakry
SIERRA LEONE
Freetown
CÔTE D'IVOIRE
GHANA
TOGO
BENIN
Abuja
Monrovia
Yamoussoukro
Porto-Novo
Lomé
Accra
LIBERIA
Addis Ababa
ETHIOPIA
SOMALIA
CENTRAL AFRICAN REPUBLIC
CAMEROON
Yaoundé
Bangui
Malabo
EQUATORIAL GUINEA
SAO TOME & PRINCIPE
São Tomé
Libreville
GABON
CONGO
Congo River
EQUATOR
UGANDA
Kampala
KENYA
Nairobi
Mogadishu
RWANDA
Kigali
DEM. REP. OF THE CONGO
BURUNDI
Bujumbura
Brazzaville
Kinshasa
CABINDA (ANGOLA)
TANZANIA
Dar es Salaam
SEYCHEL
Luanda
ANGOLA
ZAMBIA
Lusaka
Zambezi River
MALAWI
Lilongwe
MOZAMBIQUE
COMOROS
Moroni
Mozambique Channel
Harare
ZIMBABWE
Antananar
MADAGASCAR
NAMIBIA
Windhoek
BOTSWANA
Gaborone
Pretoria
Maputo
Mbabane
Maseru
Orange River
SWAZILAND
LESOTHO
SOUTH AFRICA
Cape Town
Indian Ocean
Africa
0 mi
500 mi
0 km
500 km
NATIONAL GEOGRAPHIC

Africa At A Glance

Take a look! The map and graphics on these pages give you different ways of understanding the people and cultures of Africa. The continent is home to about 840 million people living in more than 50 different countries. Africans belong to many different ethnic groups, practice many different religions, and speak many different languages. Use the map to locate each of the countries listed in the graphs and charts.

Say Hello! Hola Bon Jo

"Ahlan"	Arabic (Northern Africa)
"Jambo"	Swahili (Eastern Africa)
"Sannu"	Hausa (Western Africa)
"Mbote"	Lingala (Central Africa)
"Sawubona"	Zulu (Southern Africa)

Population of World Regions

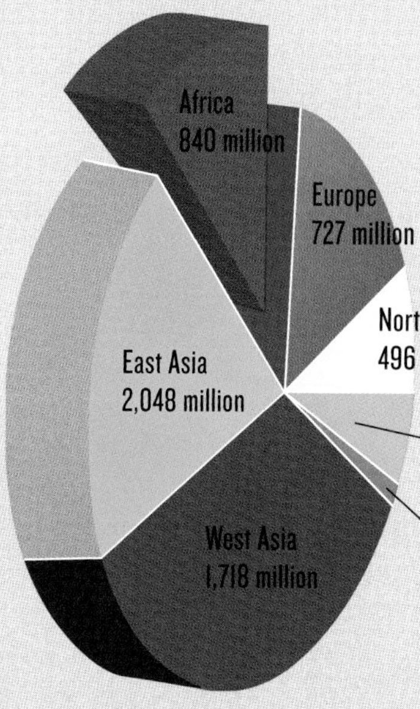

Average Income, Selected Countries of Africa

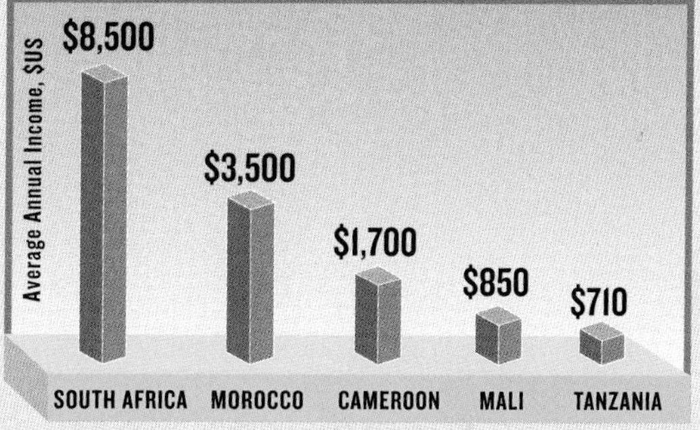

Most Populous Countries of Africa

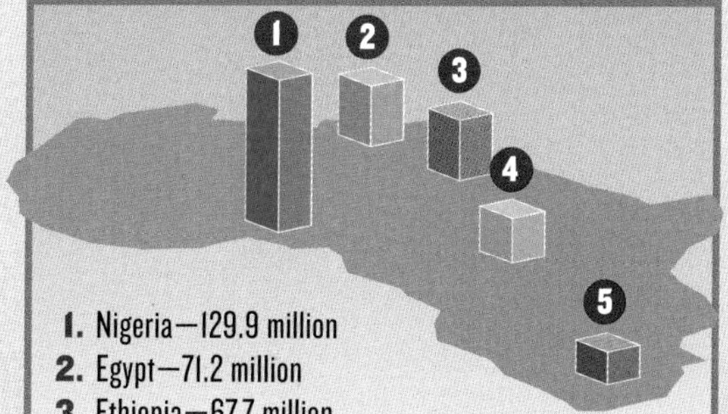

1. Nigeria—129.9 million
2. Egypt—71.2 million
3. Ethiopia—67.7 million
4. Democratic Republic of the Congo—55.2 million
5. South Africa—43.6 million

Sources

Population of World Regions: Population Reference Bureau, 2003 estimates
Most Populous African Countries: Population Reference Bureau, 2002 estimates
Average Income: 2003 World Almanac, Gross Domestic Product per person

School DAYS

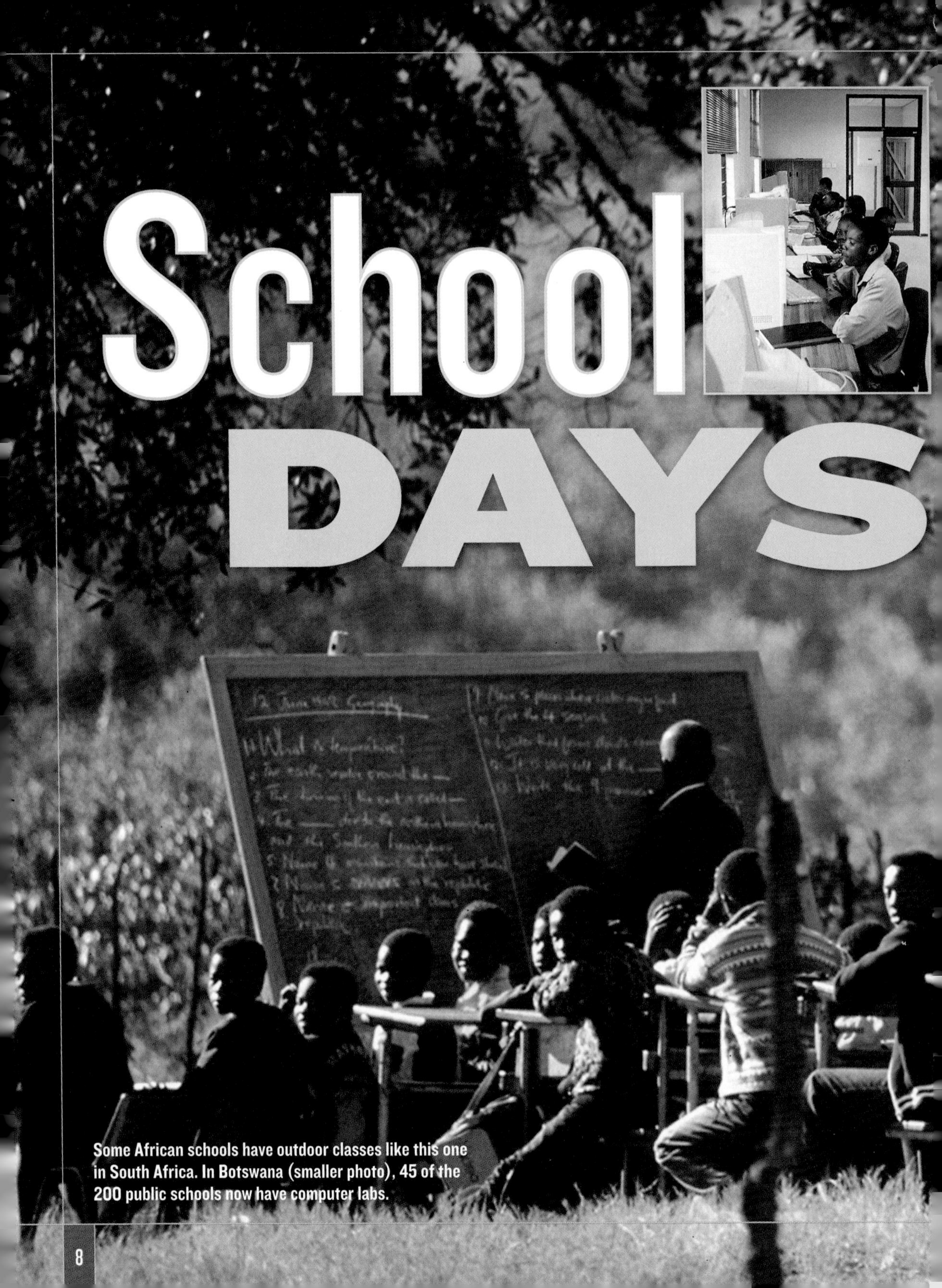

Some African schools have outdoor classes like this one in South Africa. In Botswana (smaller photo), 45 of the 200 public schools now have computer labs.

As the sun rises, students in countries throughout Africa begin getting ready for school. Like you, they head out for a new day of classes. Across Africa, children go to school for the same reason—to learn about things that will help them during their lives. But Africa is a continent of many different countries, people, languages, and religions. These differences influence education. You will see that not all schools in Africa are the same.

In some African countries students attend public schools that are usually paid for by a country's government. Some countries don't provide public education, so students have to pay for their education. Some students wear school uniforms, while some do not. Classes in Morocco are mainly taught in the Arabic language, while in Togo they are taught in French. School buildings come in all shapes and sizes. In countries with warm climates, classes can be held outside. In many poorer countries, schools have little equipment such as computers, science labs, or even writing paper or books.

Families that only have enough money to send one child to school will often send a boy rather than a girl.

Unfortunately, many children don't even go to school in Africa. In the early 2000s, only about half of all African children were enrolled in school. One reason is that African countries often do not have the money to provide free education. Public schools—which should be available for all students—may charge fees that many parents cannot afford. Parents also might not be able to afford uniforms and books needed for school.

Another reason the number of children in school is so low is that some children only attend school for a few years before they must work to help earn money for their families. Many African families still rely on farming to make a living, and all family members are needed to work on the farm.

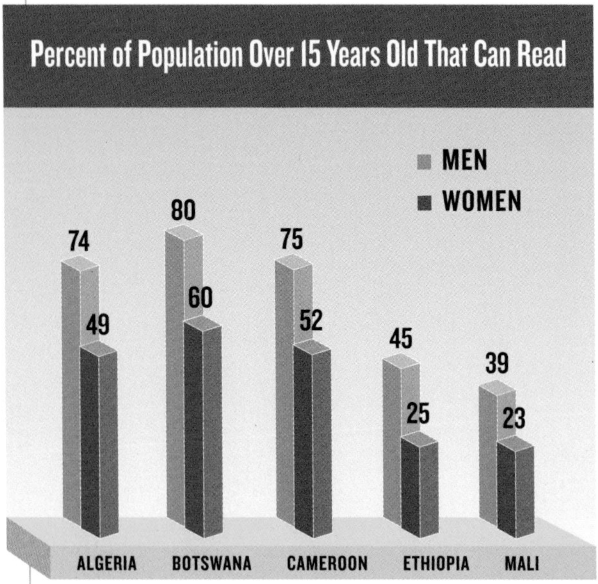

Source: CIA World Factbook, 2001

In many African countries, girls are less likely to be enrolled in school than boys. Many girls do not attend school at all, or attend only for a year or two. In some places, this happens because people believe that a girl's opportunities are at home where she can help with chores. Also, she is usually expected to marry at an early age. Families that only have enough money to send one child to school will often send a boy rather than a girl. As the chart shows, fewer girls learn to read than boys.

Education in Cameroon

In the country of Cameroon, more children learn to read than in many African countries. Although Cameroon's economy is based mainly on farming and much of the country is poor, the government does make sure that some education is free for everyone through public schools.

First grade students in Chad display tablets with their completed math problems. Idriss Deby, one of the presidents of Chad, once studied in this classroom.

In Cameroon, 71 percent of girls attend primary school, or the years of schooling before high school, compared to 82 percent of boys. Less than 25 percent of girls and about 30 percent of boys go on to attend secondary school, or high school. Primary education is free, but most secondary schools charge a fee.

One problem for education is that nearly half of Cameroon's people are under the age of 15. The country does not have enough money to build the number of schools or pay the teachers' salaries needed to educate so many children. Some areas have so few public schools that classes can have over 100 students. Even such a large class might only have one teacher.

An alternative to crowded public schools is private schools. Private schools offer smaller classes, but they are often expensive. Nearly one third of students in Cameroon go to private schools. Many of these schools are run by religious groups.

A School Day in Cameroon

It's 5:30 in the morning, and it is time for Paul to get up. First he does chores around the house. Then he gets dressed

In some schools in Morocco, children learn about the Islamic religion in addition to their other subjects. These schools are called Quranic schools.

for school and eats breakfast. After breakfast he starts his one-mile walk to school.

Paul attends a Christian high school in western Cameroon. He is in the third grade of the second phase, which is the same as ninth grade in the United States.

Paul's school has 15 classrooms, more than 300 students, a library with more than 1,000 books, and a small science laboratory. Classes are all taught in French. Students can also learn English and German. Paul has classes in math, science, and technology before a mid-morning break. Then he studies subjects such as history, geography, and civics.

After a half-hour lunch break, Paul and his classmates go back to class. They study money management and traditional arts and crafts in the afternoon. Some days Paul and the other students go outside for physical education.

When classes are finished for the day, Paul and his classmates sometimes meet in the school's library to study and do homework. On one afternoon, Paul attends English-language practice. On other days, there are club meetings for activities such as choir, theater, and sports. Sometimes the students and their teachers organize events such as field trips or dances.

A group of children walk to school in South Africa.

Schools across Africa are different from country to country, but many schools share a similar problem—lack of money and equipment.

Paul then heads home where he helps look after his younger brothers. After dinner, it's time to finish up his homework. Then it's time for bed—he'll need his rest for tomorrow!

Summing Up

Schools across Africa are different from country to country, but many schools share a similar problem—lack of money and equipment. Free public schools can be overcrowded. Private schools and many public schools can cost too much, or families need their children's help at home. Girls often receive less education than boys.

Schoolchildren visit the Rothchild Giraffe Center in Kenya where they learn about animals and the environment.

High-rise apartments and tall office buildings crowd the Cairo skyline.

CAIRO KEEPS GROWING AND GROWING

It's early in the morning, and already Egyptians in the busy capital city of Cairo are beginning their work day. Pushing their way into a crowded bus, they wait for the stop that will bring them close to their place of work. Some riders try to greet each other over the rush and noise of traffic.

Cairo is an example of an African city that is growing in size and population. Only about one-third of Africa's people live in **urban** areas now, but this number is increasing. Why? Cities are growing as more and more Africans are moving to them for better jobs and education. As cities grow quickly, however, there are many challenges for people and governments in these urban areas.

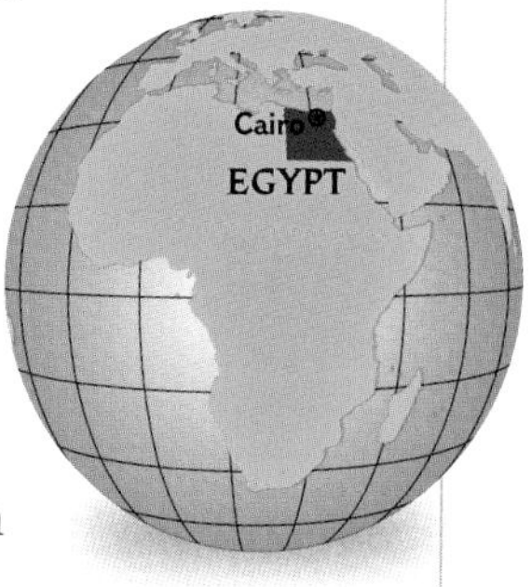

In the early 1900s, about 95 percent of Africans lived in **rural** areas where most people were farmers or herders. Gradually the **migration,** or movement, of people from rural to urban areas began, and cities grew larger. This growth of city population, or **urbanization,** continues today. It is estimated that by 2010, more than 40 percent of Africans will live in cities. What does this mean for the city of Cairo, Egypt?

Most people in rural Egypt make their living by farming and selling their goods in village markets.

Migration to Cairo

About 30 million people—that's slightly less than half of Egypt's population—now live in or near cities. More than 10 million of these people currently live in and around Cairo. People continue to migrate to big cities like Cairo from rural Egypt. Why do people move to cities? What would it be like to move from a rural part of Egypt to the bustling capital city?

Rural Life

First, let's look at what rural life is like in Egypt. Before 6 a.m., the farmers of Egypt's rural villages are awake for the first meal of the day before heading to the fields. In communities close to the Nile River, farmers raise crops such as cotton, dates, corn, and sugarcane.

Villages often have a lively market where people buy and sell food, animals, tools, clothing, and other goods. People also go to the market to meet friends and exchange news. Most villages also have a mosque, or Muslim place of worship.

After a long day of working in the fields, tending to their animals, cooking, cleaning, and visiting the market, family members share a meal. Families often live in small houses made with mud bricks. Some houses have electricity while others are lit by oil lamps. Water is usually available from a well shared by everyone in the community.

Many of Cairo's streets stay busy and filled with people.

Life in Cairo

A farmer from rural Egypt arriving in Cairo for the first time might be overwhelmed by the sights, sounds, and smells of the city. The streets of Cairo are packed with cars, buses, bicycles, donkey carts, and lots of people. Some might be selling newspapers, while others are hurrying to work. Others might be sitting at one of Cairo's hundreds of outdoor cafes having coffee. The air is thick with dust, pollution, and noise.

Gone are the small houses of the Nile villages. Cairo is full of high-rise apartment buildings, where most city residents live. Buildings are crowded close together. Many apartments have electricity and running water.

Like people all over the world, Cairo's people work at a wide range of jobs. Most businesses close for a few hours in the afternoon for a break. Then workers return to their jobs and work into the evening. Dinnertime can be as late as 10 p.m.

While their parents work, many children spend the day in school taking subjects such as math, history, geography, and music. There are also four large universities in Cairo.

The streets of Cairo are packed with cars, buses, bicycles, donkey carts, and lots of people.

Push and Pull Factors

Why do people migrate from rural areas to large cities such as Cairo? Farmers depend on a good harvest each year, but sometimes a lack of rainfall or a plant disease can destroy a crop. A poor harvest is an example of a **push factor**, or something that causes a person to migrate from one place to another. Another push factor is the limited amount of land available for farming. Only about 4 percent of the land in Egypt can be used for farming, and the population is growing rapidly. Other push factors include a lack of jobs outside of farming and poor educational opportunities.

As problems "push" some Egyptians from rural areas, Cairo and other Egyptian cities attract them with what they have to offer. These attractions are **pull factors.** Cairo and other cities "pull" rural people with the potential of a wide variety of jobs and better educational opportunities. Often, however, people find that the opportunities are not as promising as they had thought.

Push and Pull of Migration

PUSH FACTORS FROM RURAL AREAS

- Difficult work
- Poor education
- Lack of jobs

PULL FACTORS TO URBAN AREAS

- Wide variety of jobs
- Better education
- Better transportation

More than 150,000 students attend Cairo University.

Nearly one million people live among the tombs in the "City of the Dead."

Pull factors have special significance for women. Most women in rural areas still have traditional duties of farming and taking care of the home. In the past, few women went to school and learned skills for jobs outside the home, but more and more women are finding education for careers as teachers, lawyers, or doctors in the cities. Today, about 20 percent of women in Cairo have jobs outside the home.

Growth Causes Problems

Cairo and other large cities offer opportunities for people, but like in many cities around the world, growing population has caused problems. Finding good housing is one problem. People often crowd into small apartments with many other relatives. Others must sleep outside. Cairo is so crowded that one community was built on top of a cemetery. Known as the "City of the Dead," the area is dotted with homes squeezed among the tombs.

Cairo faces other challenges. The abundance of industry and automobiles in the city has polluted Cairo's air. Not all people have water, electricity, and good waste disposal. There is also a shortage of jobs for those who come to the city. The people of Cairo are searching for ways to solve these problems.

Summing Up

All across Africa, people are migrating from rural areas to cities in record numbers. Cities like Cairo offer many opportunities, including a better education and a wider variety of jobs. Despite the opportunities, large cities face challenges. Cairo and other cities are trying to find ways to solve the problems that come with overcrowding, such as air pollution, lack of housing, and a strained supply of water and electricity.

Chinua Achebe

Chinua Achebe (below) is a well-known Nigerian writer whose books are read all over the world. Much of his writing describes what life is like for the Igbo people of southeastern Nigeria. ▪ *Chike and the River* is one of Achebe's novels for children. It tells the story of Chike, a young boy who moves from a rural village to a large city. Chike and his family experience the "push" and "pull" factors that many people have felt when moving from a small village or town to a big city.

Chike lived with his mother and two sisters in the village of Umuofia. His father had died many years ago. His mother worked very hard to feed and clothe her three children and to send them to school. She grew most of the food they ate—yams, cassava, maize, beans, plantains, and many green vegetables. She also traded in dry fish, palm-oil, kerosene and matches.

Chike was now eleven years old, and he never left his

village. Then one day his mother told him that he would be going to Onitsha in the new year to live with his uncle who was a clerk in one of the firms there. At first Chike was full of joy. He was tired of living in a bush village and wanted to see a big city. He had heard many wonderful stories about Onitsha. His uncle's servant, Michael, had told him that there was a water-tap in the very compound where they lived. Chike said this was impossible, but Michael had sworn to its truth by wetting his first finger on his tongue and pointing it to the sky. Chike was too thrilled for words. So he would no longer wake up early in the morning to go to the stream. The trouble with their village stream was that the way to it was very rough and stony, and sometimes children fell and broke their waterpots. In Onitsha Chike would be free from all those worries. Also he would live in a house with an iron roof instead of his mother's poor hut of mud and thatch. It all sounded so wonderful.

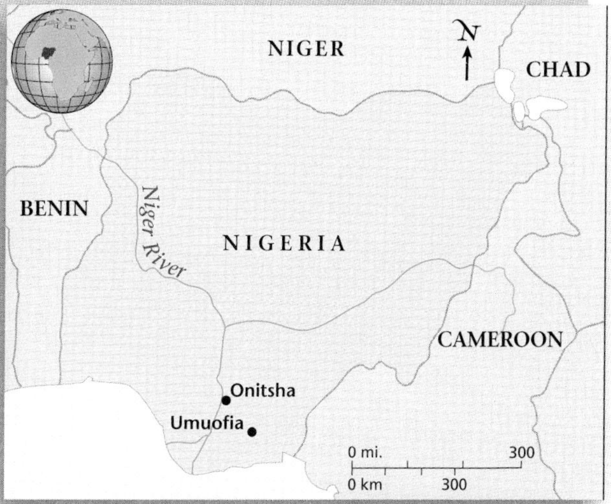

But when the time actually came for Chike to leave his mother and sisters he began to cry. His sisters cried too, and even his mother had signs of tears in her eyes. She placed one hand on his head and said: "Go well, my son. Listen to whatever your uncle says and obey him. Onitsha is a big city . . ."

"He was tired of living in a bush village and wanted to see a big city."

A Health Crisis

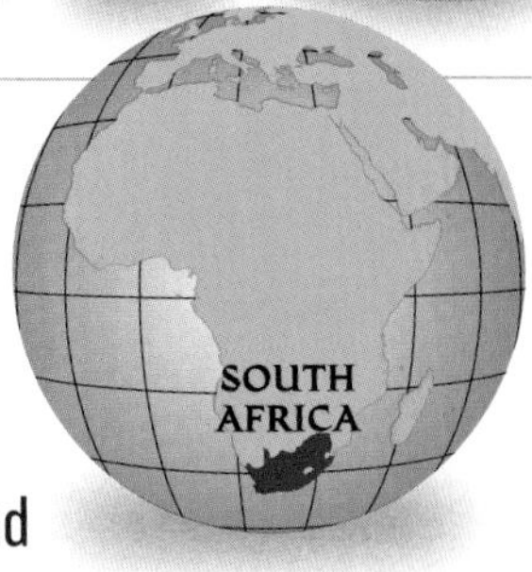

Concerns about health problems exist in many parts of Africa. Some areas lack clean drinking water. Others lack a steady supply of food. There are often not enough doctors or medical supplies to provide all residents with good health care. Tropical diseases such as malaria and sleeping sickness affect millions of people.

Children in South Africa join the fight against the spread of AIDS.

One of the most serious health problems in Africa today is AIDS. AIDS is a deadly disease caused by the HIV virus. More than 70 percent of the people infected with HIV/AIDS in the world live in Africa.

The country of South Africa has one of the most serious AIDS problems in the world. It is nearly impossible not to be aware of AIDS in South Africa. Students attend educational programs about the disease. Newspapers print articles about the problems caused by HIV/AIDS. Billboards explaining how to stop the spread of the disease hang in South African cities.

AIDS is particularly hard on children. In 2001, there were 660,000 children living in South Africa who had lost a parent to AIDS, and the number is growing. A 12-year-old girl who lives near Johannesburg described life with family members who have AIDS:

"*My mother is very sick. After school, I have to take care of my baby brother and my mother. Sometimes I don't get enough sleep and fall off to sleep in class . . . My thoughts are always with my brother and mother because they have AIDS.*"

Getting the Word Out

Since there is no cure for AIDS, the best way to fight the disease is to prevent people from getting it. Education is essential to stopping the spread of AIDS.

There are many different AIDS education programs in South Africa. Kanthee Raidoo is one of many South Africans who teach others about AIDS prevention. Raidoo and a team of educators travel from school to school in the city of Durban. Their educational group is called Phakama, which means "rise up" in the Zulu language.

TECH TALK Soul Buddyz

Television is another tool that is being used to educate people about AIDS and other health issues. *Soul Buddyz* is a popular South African television show geared toward young people that follows the adventures of a group of friends as they face different issues. *Soul Buddyz* is entertainment, but it also aims to teach kids how to take care of themselves.

Soul Buddyz cast members

Raidoo and other members of Phakama perform a play about AIDS. Then they answer questions from the student audiences. Raidoo hopes that with each school they visit, more students will gain the information they need to prevent the spread of the disease.

Students Join the Fight

Many students are getting the message from programs like Raidoo's and are starting to take action themselves. Thirteen-year-old Kamohelo Mabula traveled to Spain with five other South African students to attend the World AIDS Conference in Barcelona, Spain, in 2002. There he learned more about health and how he could help educate his fellow students. "My involvement in the conference," he said, "has made me realize that there is a great need for youth to actively participate in the fighting of HIV/AIDS."

Percentage of World AIDS Cases by Continent

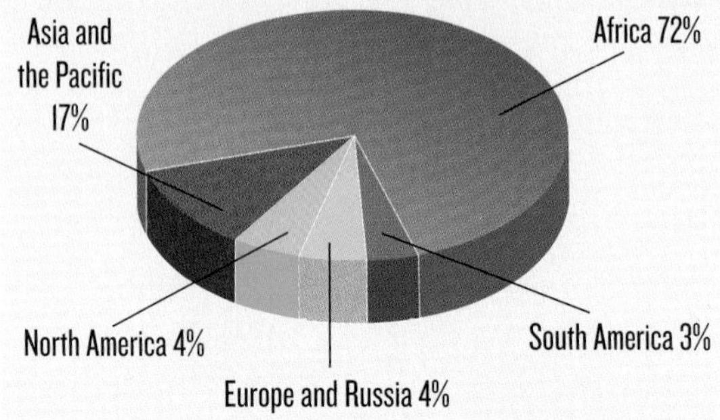

Source: The UNAIDS/WHO Working Group on Global HIV/AIDS and STI Surveillance

Former South African president Nelson Mandela visits an AIDS care center.

College students across South Africa are also becoming more involved in the fight against AIDS. In July 2002, nearly 4,000 students held a march in the city of Johannesburg to raise awareness. College students also run workshops, help students get free testing for the HIV virus, and make posters teaching about AIDS.

Treating People

Although education programs are helping to raise awareness about AIDS, there are still more than four million people in South Africa living with the disease. No one has found a cure for AIDS yet, but there are medicines that

can help ease symptoms and extend the lives of people with AIDS. These medicines are expensive, and many South Africans cannot afford them. The government has been unable to provide medicines to everyone who needs them.

How can patients get the medicine they need? Many international organizations are setting up programs to help distribute AIDS medicines. Some employers in South Africa are beginning to help, as well. In 2002, a large mining company began to provide AIDS medication for workers infected with the virus.

▲ **AIDS is a problem all over the world. People attending the 2002 World AIDS Conference in Barcelona, Spain, hold a candlelight vigil.**

Summing Up

Health problems are a concern in many parts of Africa. AIDS is one problem, especially in certain countries like South Africa. Education may be the best weapon in the fight against this deadly disease. Students and many others are dedicating their lives to educating South Africans about the disease. In schools, in the workplace, and even on television, the facts about AIDS are being delivered. Organizations in the country and from all over the world are helping people with AIDS get the medicines they need, but prevention is still the best cure.

Sculpting in Stone

Throughout Africa, people have developed varied artistic traditions. They create art using materials such as colorful cloth, wood, and painted beads. Recently, a new artistic tradition has developed. Artists in places like Chapungu Sculpture Park in Harare, Zimbabwe, are now creating huge, powerful stone sculptures that are admired all over the world. These artists are giving a special meaning to the name of their country, Zimbabwe, which means "house of stone."

Although Chapungu Sculpture Park opened only about 30 years ago, stone sculpting has been a tradition in Zimbabwe for centuries. The country was named for an area of giant stone ruins known as Great Zimbabwe. These ruins are the remains of a trading city that thrived for more than 1,000 years, until about 1500.

Chapungu Sculpture Park covers 15 acres of beautiful gardens. Wander through Chapungu, and you will find yourself surrounded by stones carved to look like animals, people, and even spirits. You may also find yourself surrounded by the sculptors themselves, practicing their craft in the open air.

Zimbabwean sculptor Colleen Madamombe carved this sculpture which she calls "Growing Well."

Making the Sculptures

How do Chapungu artists make their sculptures? They begin by traveling to different parts of Zimbabwe to find the stone themselves. Many artists get their stones from a stretch of hills west of the capital city of Harare. Artists look for different types of stone. Springstone, for example, is a very hard, gray stone that looks black when polished. Artists dig the stone from the hills and transport it back to Chapungu. Some of the chunks of stone can weigh more than 6,000 pounds!

Artists then begin to chip away at the stone to reveal a shape. They use only hand tools, such as a hammer and a chisel. When it is time to create details, artists might use a file and a chasing, a tool with comb teeth, to create texture and lines.

Finally, artists use a very fine sandpaper to smooth out the stone, and then a beeswax polish to add shine. Not all areas of the sculpture are sanded down and polished, though. Having both rough and sanded areas can make the sculptures more interesting and lifelike.

The sculpting process can take a very long time, depending on the size and hardness of the stone and how complicated the design is. It often takes up to a year to complete a single sculpture.

Finding the Meaning

There are as many ideas represented in the sculptures as there are individual artists. Each sculpture reflects the themes of its artist's beliefs and experiences. Many artists are Shona, the largest ethnic group in Zimbabwe. Shona artists often represent Shona traditions and spiritual beliefs in their sculptures. For example, the word "Chapungu" means "eagle" in the Shona language. The Shona people believe that the eagle can carry spiritual messages, so they often represent them in stone sculptures.

Artist Colleen Madamombe uses sculptures, like the one on page 26, to portray the lives of women in the changing society of Zimbabwe. Madamombe is glad that women now have opportunities to explore careers. Yet she also believes that things should not change completely. She wants to remind women that there is power and joy in the traditional roles of mother and homemaker.

Sylvester Mubayi's sculpture, "Protected By Spirits," reflects the importance of family in Shona culture.

Many of Great Zimbabwe's structures still stand today, proving that Zimbabweans have been skilled stoneworkers for hundreds of years.

Summing Up

Chapungu Sculpture Park is one example of the thriving tradition of art in Africa. The stone sculptures created there have been exhibited in many parts of the world, including the United States. Artists who work at the park carve the sculptures by hand. The culture of the artists influences the meaning of their sculptures.

James Lovemore

James Lovemore begins work on a new sculpture. (Upper right) Lovemore hides behind his sculpture called "Chapungu and the Lady."

My name is James Lovemore.

I am a sculptor at Chapungu Sculpture Park in Zimbabwe. There are many people looking for jobs in Zimbabwe, so I feel lucky to have a job as a sculptor. I sculpt because I want to be a successful artist, but also to feed my wife and children and pay the school fees. In my sculptures I tell stories of my background and what is happening in my life so that people who come to Zimbabwe can understand me.

Every morning I drink my tea and eat my bread so that I am fit to make my sculptures. I jump into my old yellow car and head to Chapungu. The park is in the city, but it is a piece of African bush with friendly monkeys that leap around like dancers and watch us make sculptures. They even sit on our sculptures!

I have to check in each morning like all employed people. I must be there by 8 A.M. After I check in, I open my tool kit, in which I have a hammer, chisel, and file, each cleaned the night before.

Today I am working on a sculpture I call "Chapungu and the Lady." On one side, there is an eagle with a massive beak, strong talons [claws], and a wide wingspan. On the other side you can see an elegant African lady with a beautiful nose and wonderful hair. I start to work on the stone. The air is full of noise—hammers, visitors, and another noise—the music of my cell phone. My wife has called to ask if I could bring some relish home to eat with our sadza, which is maize meal.

I see the visitors looking at my sculpture and smiling. Maybe they will buy it so that my wife can have a good sewing machine and my grandmother can get the medicine she needs. I spend the rest of my day filing this sculpture.

I leave Chapungu at 5 P.M. I drive home in my old yellow car, bumping on the dirt road. When I get there I greet my wife and child and we eat our sadza with the relish I bought. Then I go to sleep and dream of the next sculpture I will create.

Lovemore has just completed a new sculpture he calls "Life Pattern."

Going the Distance

Kenyan Catherine Ndereba crosses the finish line, winning the 2000 Boston Marathon.

In the highlands near Mount Kenya, the air is thin and the trails are difficult. None of this stops the determined Kenyan runners who train there. Some of these runners will go on to participate in races all over the world. And, as history has shown, they have a good chance of winning.

Many of the world's top runners come from Kenya. In fact, Kenyan men and women dominate long-distance running, especially **marathons.** A marathon is a foot race over a course that is 26.2 miles (42 kilometers) long. Kenyan men won a major marathon in Boston, Massachusetts—the Boston Marathon—10 years in a row, from 1991–2000.

Kenyan women are also successful marathon runners. One Kenyan runner, Catherine Ndereba (dah RAY bah), won four major marathons in just two years—in 2000 and 2001. Male and female runners have brought pride to their country and have inspired many future Kenyan athletes.

Secrets to Success

Many Kenyans start running at a very young age. One example is Cosmas Ndeti (DEH tee). Born in the town of Machakos, he began running to school because he often woke up late. Soon he began to love running and started training more seriously.

Like many Kenyan runners, Ndeti trained at high **altitudes.** Altitude is the height of the land above sea level. At high altitudes, the air is thinner, making it more difficult for people to breathe when they exercise. Many runners and their trainers believe that high-altitude training helps runners strengthen their lungs so they can run long distances with less effort.

Ndeti trained by running for two to three hours along rough trails around Mount Kenya at an altitude of 6,500 feet (1,981 meters). He covered more than 20 miles in that time! Ndeti's hard training paid off. He won the Boston Marathon three years in a row—1993, 1994, and 1995.

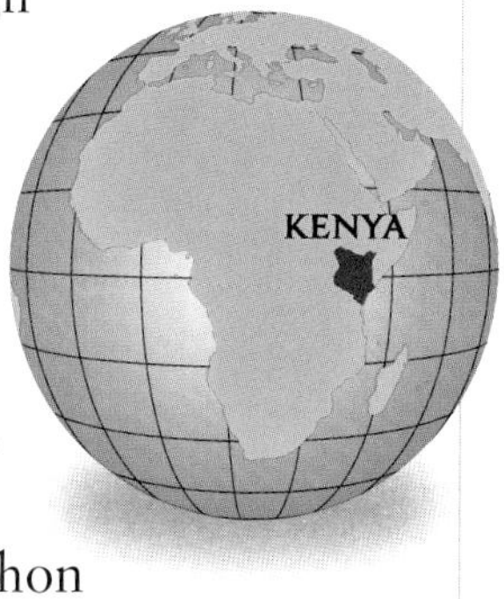

Women Crossing the Finish Line

Women in Kenya—as in many parts of the world—have not always been encouraged to become athletes. In traditional Kenyan society, women are

...Kenyan women began to compete in international races in the 1970s, and their success inspired more women to challenge tradition.

expected to take care of their home and children. But Kenyan women began to compete in international races in the 1970s, and their success inspired more women to challenge tradition.

One of the best known Kenyan runners is Catherine Ndereba. In the 2001 Chicago Marathon, she broke the world record for women marathon runners. She finished the race in 2 hours, 18 minutes, and 47 seconds.

Ndereba's husband supports her running and takes care of their daughter, Jane, while Ndereba competes. Some Kenyans might disapprove of this arrangement, but others believe it will continue to open up opportunities for women.

Giving Back to the Community

The success that Kenyan athletes have found in running can significantly change their lives and the lives of their families and communities. For example, Ndereba received $80,000 for her first place finish in the 2001 Boston Marathon. She has used some of the money she won from this and other races to pay for her brothers and sisters to go to school. She has also started a race in her hometown of Nyeri to help discover young runners.

Another Kenyan marathon winner, Lornah Kiplagat, used the money she won to build a training camp for women runners in Kenya. Kenyan girls train there for free. The goal of the camp, says Kiplagat's husband, is not "to give [the girls] a running career. Just a career. A future."

Summing Up

Kenyan men and women are known all over the world for their success in long-distance running. They train hard, often in the mountains, and work toward being the very best. Their success has brought excitement and pride to the nation. As more women break world records and win races, some attitudes about the role of women in Kenyan society are changing. Successful runners have helped their families and communities.

Meet El Hadji Diouf of Senegal

Kenyan runners are not the only Africans making headlines in international sports. In 2002, Senegalese fans of football—called soccer in the United States—were thrilled to watch their team qualify for the World Cup for the first time in Senegal's history. The Lions of Teranga unexpectedly defeated France in the first round and Sweden in the second. They made it all the way to the quarterfinals, becoming the first African team to make it that far since Cameroon did it in 1990.

El Hadji Diouf (joof), 21 years old, was a major part of the team's success. Wearing number 11 and playing forward, Diouf scored in eight out of the nine qualifying games for Senegal.

Diouf signed with a professional team in France when he was only 17 years old. In the few years he has been a professional athlete, he has earned many honors. He was named the 2001 African Footballer of the Year. He also made the 2002 World Cup All-Star Team.

Diouf was asked how he and the other players felt about bringing the Senegalese team all the way to the World Cup quarterfinals. "That has given us and the people back home extraordinary pleasure," he said. "We are happy that we made the quarterfinals. Africa is proud of us."

A Tale of Two Weddings

In Africa, as in every region of the world, traditions are a very important part of life. People stay connected to their heritage and culture through traditional gatherings such as birthday observances, religious celebrations, and weddings. ■ Weddings are a chance to blend the old and the new. The bride and groom are starting a new marriage and a new life together. Yet they want to carry on the traditions they have learned from their families and communities.

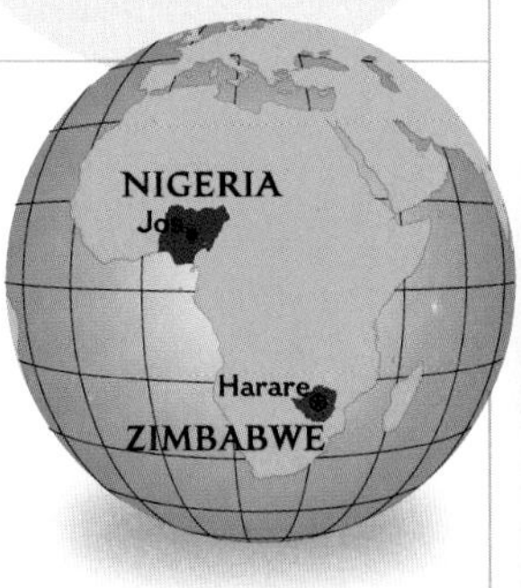

Chenai Karimakwenda and George Okammor know a lot about blending old and new traditions. In fact, they wanted to celebrate so many traditions when they got married that they actually planned two weddings!

Chenai was born in Harare, Zimbabwe. A member of the Shona, she had grown up following their customs. Chenai moved to the United States when she was 12 years old. Soon she became used to many American ways of doing things. When she was 21, she started traveling back to Zimbabwe every summer to visit her family. "I became more conscious of who I really was," she says. "Not all American—not all African."

Getting Started

While living in Chicago, Illinois, Chenai met George Okammor. George is from Jos, Nigeria. He is a member of the Igbo ethnic group of southeastern Nigeria. He came to the United States at the age of 18.

One day George cooked Chenai an African meal. Chenai was surprised and

George and Chenai held their traditional wedding at the home of Chenai's mother in Harare.

impressed. She sat down and started eating with her hands in the traditional African way, like it was the most natural thing in the world. Then *he* was surprised! Four months later, they were engaged to be married.

Chenai wanted to return to her mother's home in Zimbabwe for the wedding. She knew that in her wedding she wanted to honor the diverse cultures and traditions in her life. There were many other decisions to be made. For example, George and Chenai wanted to find a way to include both Shona and Igbo traditions in their wedding. Also, since both George and Chenai are Christian, they wanted to include Christian traditions as well.

Twice the Celebration

The solution? Chenai and George had two wedding days. On the first day, they were married in a Christian ceremony in downtown Harare. The ceremony was in three languages—English, Shona, and Igbo. Chenai wore a white wedding dress and walked down the center aisle to meet George. After the ceremony, the guests were invited to a sit-down lunch in a hotel.

This was just the beginning. On the second day, Chenai and George had a traditional African celebration at the home of Chenai's mother in Harare. Chenai explains, "Weddings are supposed to be for the whole community. Everyone who has ever known your mother and father, or anyone who has ever known you from the day you were born is entitled to come!"

Chenai and George wore brightly colored traditional Igbo clothes. George also wore a red cap, which Igbo men wear only on very special occasions. The wedding included traditional Shona drumming and dancing, and lots of eating. Ceremonial speeches were given by people close to the couple, which is a Shona tradition.

George and Chenai dance at their Christian wedding celebration.

Meet Alice Wangui of Kenya

Alice Wangui and her son Scott walk through the village where they were born.

Although it is almost time for the baby's birth, Alice Wangui of Kenya is traveling 90 miles on a bus over bumpy roads with her seven-year-old son, Scott. She is returning to Nyeri—the village where she was born, and where Scott was born.

Wangui owns a successful hair salon in Nairobi, the capital of Kenya. There, she could have her baby in a hospital. But like many Africans, Wangui feels very strongly about the traditions of her people. "You're supposed to give birth where you were born," she says. "It's very important. You are supposed to go back to your home."

Wangui's people, the Kikuyu, live in eastern Kenya. Her grandfather and father were born in the village she calls home. "I want my children to follow the culture and know where they come from," she says.

Summing Up

Weddings and other traditional ceremonies are an important part of cultures in Africa and all over the world. Ceremonies are often a blend of old and new traditions, as well as several cultures. It sometimes takes a lot more planning to combine different religions and cultures. Many people like George, Chenai, and Alice believe it is worth the effort to honor both their heritage and new ways of life.

Growing Up MASAI

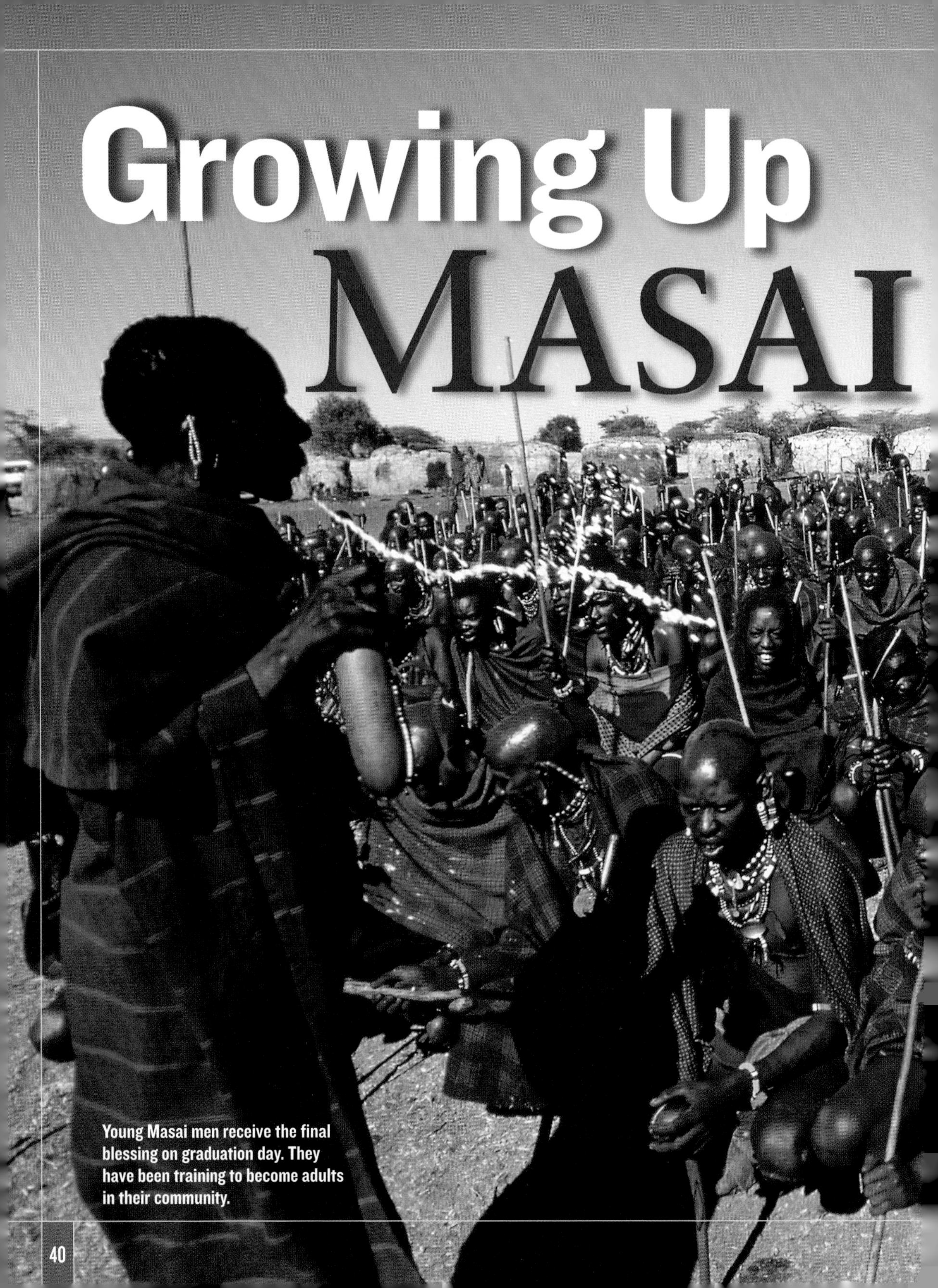

Young Masai men receive the final blessing on graduation day. They have been training to become adults in their community.

TRADITIONS

Growing up means taking on new responsibilities. Most African cultures have a traditional ceremony to honor young people who are becoming adults in the eyes of the community. The Masai people, who live in Kenya and Tanzania, have a very special ceremony in which young men become adults. It is one of the most important events of their lives.

Traditionally, the Masai way of life is based on cattle. The Masai have long moved from place to place across the East African grasslands as they herd and graze their cattle. Today most Masai live in cities, but some still follow traditional ways of life. Often young Masai men, especially those living in rural areas, celebrate their adulthood with a ceremony called **Eunoto** (yoo NOH toh).

Young Masai men are traditionally called warriors, or **morans** (mohr AHNZ). They become morans when they are in their teens. Morans learn how to hunt and protect their families. They grow their hair long and color it red. The red color is used to show that the morans are energetic and spirited.

After about 10 years as a moran, young Masai men are considered ready to become adults. It is at this time that they participate in the week-long Eunoto ceremony. Hundreds of Masai march to the ceremony, sometimes walking for several days to get there.

Preparing for Adulthood

To prepare for the Eunoto ceremony, mothers of the morans build a circle of structures called a **manyatta** (man YAHT uh). This is where the ceremony takes place. Inside one of the structures, a fire is built that must burn for the entire ceremony. Several women are responsible for making sure the fire does not go out.

Before marching to the ceremony site, the morans trade their hunting spears for walking sticks. This shows that each young man will trade the life of a warrior for that of an adult. One of the first things the young men

Warriors wear necklaces such as the one above. A moran (below) blows a ceremonial horn called a Kudu horn.

The red color is used to show the morans are energetic and spirited.

do after their arrival is use a special white chalk to paint their bodies. Sometimes they paint pictures that tell stories, such as what happened during an important hunt. The young men then receive special blessings. Later in the ceremony, they run around the manyatta that contains the fire. They run faster and faster. Some of the morans blow horns as they circle the manyatta. There is dancing, singing, and chanting.

Morans paint themselves with white chalk at the beginning of the ceremony.

New Responsibilities

When the sun rises on the last day of the Eunoto ceremony, each moran's mother shaves off his long hair. Afterward, the men burst into an energetic dance which shows that although they are now adults, the Masai men are still spirited.

Now that they are adults, they will be expected to marry, have children, and raise cattle. They also will be expected to think and act like adults. They receive this advice: "Now that you are an adult, drop your weapons and use your head and wisdom instead."

Changing Way of Life

The Eunoto ceremony is an ancient tradition. While it is still celebrated by some Masai, their way of life is changing. Even Masai who do learn how to hunt cannot practice all of the traditional warrior duties. For example, hunting lions—once an important task of a warrior—is now against the law.

Summing Up

Although the way of life has changed for many Masai, some communities still celebrate traditional ceremonies, such as Eunoto. The Eunoto ceremony celebrates the time when a Masai male becomes an adult.

Science on the Farm

About two-thirds of Africa's people are farmers. But in some parts of the continent, poor soil, hot temperatures, and little rainfall make farming difficult. In addition, insects can destroy crops, and plant diseases can ruin a whole farm. ■ In Kenya, more than 80 percent of the country's 31 million people depend on farming to make a living. But much of Kenya's land is very dry. Only about 12 percent of the land is good for farming. The area of fertile land is very crowded, so the soil is overused and loses nutrients. Crop diseases spread quickly. Problems such as these have led to decreased crop production. Kenyans have turned to new technology to help them grow more and healthier crops.

What kind of technology could help Kenyan farmers? **Biotechnology** came to their rescue. Biotechnology is the use of science and technology to modify, or change, living things. Using biotechnology, scientists have been able to change the way certain plants grow. These changed plants can sometimes resist plant diseases, survive insects, and grow with little water. Scientists

Scientist Florence Wambugu works with farmers in Kenya to find ways to raise stronger crops that resist disease.

can even change a plant so it produces more food. Not everyone thinks biotechnology is the best solution for Africa's farming problems, but it has helped increase the production of some crops since the mid-1990s.

A Better Bunch of Bananas

One important Kenyan crop that has benefited from biotechnology is the banana. Many Kenyan farmers grow bananas for a living. Bananas, a good source of vitamins and minerals, are also grown by farmers as food for their own families.

Africa produces about 35 percent of the world's bananas.

In the late 1980s and early 1990s, many farmers realized that plants were producing fewer bananas each year. Plant diseases and insects had begun to destroy more and more crops. Farmers needed help.

Scientists went to work to find a way to help Kenya's banana farmers. Working with healthy banana plants in a laboratory, scientists discovered how to make bananas grow much faster. They also found ways to grow more plants using a section, or shoot, of one plant. This type of biotechnology is called **tissue culture.** Normally one banana shoot could produce about 10 plants in six months. Using tissue culture, scientists could make a banana shoot produce 2,000 plants in the same amount of time! And the process used to grow the new banana plants made them more resistant to drought and insects.

Bringing It to the Farm

In 1997, the Kenya Agricultural Research Institute decided to try using these plants on more farms. Now banana farmers are able to grow four to five times more bananas on the same amount of land. This is especially important since many Kenyan farmers only have small plots of farmland. Today Kenya can help feed its own people and also strengthen its economy by selling to other countries.

A New Type of Rice, Sierra Leone

Monty Jones examines a rice plant.

Biotechnology is also helping West Africa, where many farmers grow rice. In this part of Africa, rice has become a regular and important part of people's diets. But traditional African types of rice plants often do not produce enough rice to feed most families. An Asian type of rice plant, brought to Africa more than 400 years ago, grows more rice, but weeds and insects make it difficult for farmers to grow. Because they need more rice, West Africans have had to buy it from other countries.

To solve the West African rice problem, a scientist from Sierra Leone named Monty Jones created a new type of rice in 1991. Jones combined rice plants from Asia and Africa to give the new rice the best qualities of each. The new type of rice is called Nerica. This name comes from the phrase "New Rice for Africa." Like the African rice plant, Nerica resists weeds and insects. It also produces more rice like the Asian rice plant.

In the late 1990s and early 2000s several countries, including Côte d'Ivoire (koht dee VWAHR), Guinea, and Togo started programs to bring the new rice to farmers. The programs have been successful, and it is hoped that Nerica can be used by even more farmers in upcoming years.

Concerns About Biotechnology

Not everyone thinks biotechnology is the best answer for farming problems in Kenya and the rest of the world. Some people think it is too early to know whether altered plants, such as Kenya's special bananas, are safe to eat. They worry that the new types of foods may have harmful effects on people. Others worry about how the new crops could affect the environment. They believe that the soil, water, and even air could be changed by coming into contact with altered plant types.

Another problem is cost. Biotechnology programs are expensive. Therefore, farmers must pay more for the new plants than for ordinary plants.

Summing Up

Although not everyone supports it, biotechnology is making its way onto Kenyan farms, as well as farms in other countries across Africa. Scientists have been able to produce new varieties of food plants, such as bananas and rice, that can withstand harsh climates and resist insects and disease. They also grow faster and produce more food on the same amount of land. Over time, this biotechnology may help to reduce hunger and poverty in Africa.

Global Candy

Technology doesn't just help crops grow. It also helps turn crops into the kinds of foods you see every day. Some farmers in Africa grow cacao beans. The chocolate bar with almonds that you buy at your local store is made from cacao beans. Cacao must be processed with several other ingredients before it can become chocolate.

The raw ingredients for chocolate are grown in many different countries. They are then processed into candy in high-tech factories.

Cacao beans are gathered from trees near the Equator. Approximately 40 percent of the world's cacao comes from the West African country of Côte d'Ivoire.

Sugar to sweeten chocolate is processed from sugarcane and sugar beets. Major exporters of sugar are found on nearly every continent.

Finally, the cacao beans are processed into cocoa butter and are mixed with other ingredients, such as almonds, in factories located mainly in Western Europe and North America. The exact process and the proportions of ingredients are usually closely guarded secrets.

Cacao beans

A Belgian chocolate factory

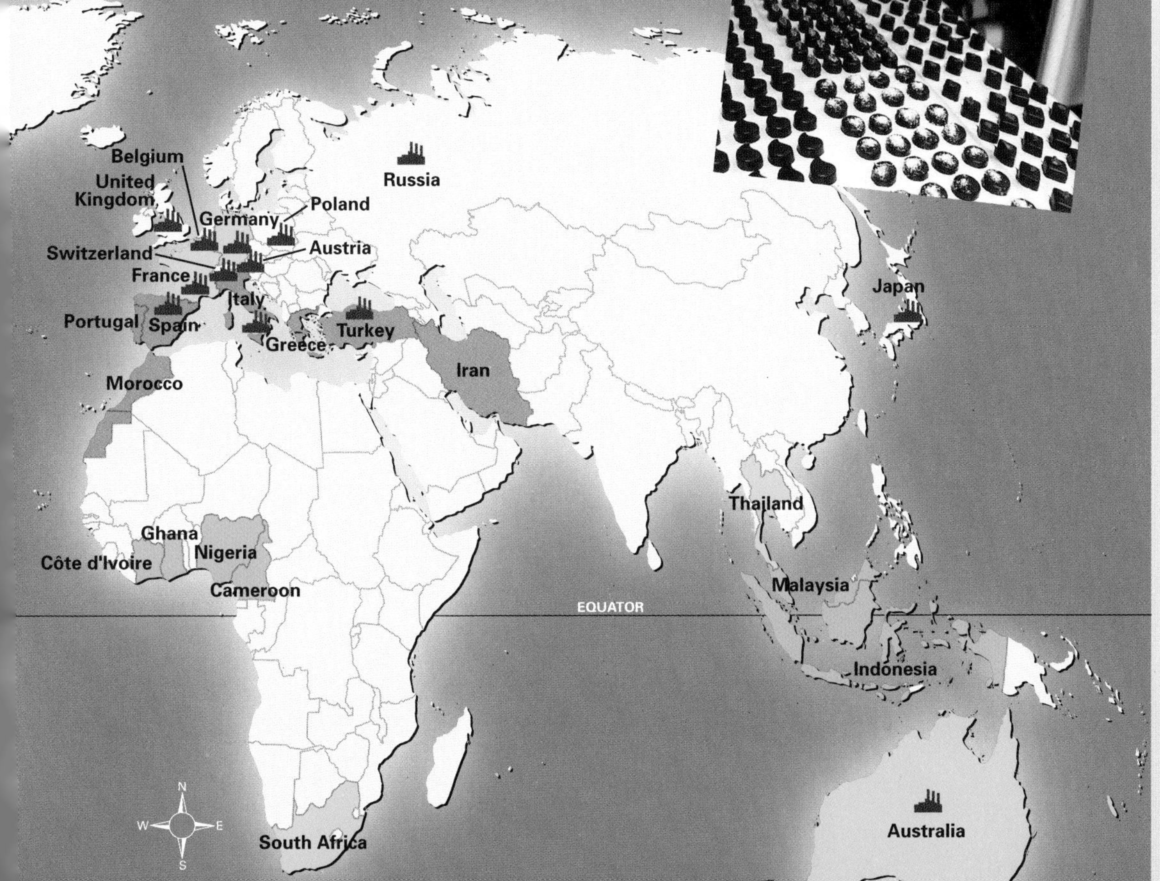

Workers split cacao pods in Côte d'Ivoire.

Oil in Nigeria

Several countries in Africa are rich in oil. No country on the continent, however, produces more oil than Nigeria. In fact, it is one of the top oil producers in the world. The production of oil brings many benefits to Nigeria. It also brings some problems.

Workers tend to an oil rig in Nigeria.

Oil is important to Nigeria. It makes up over 90 percent of Nigeria's **exports,** or products sold to other countries. Large international companies also pay Nigeria's government to be able to drill inside the country. Most of the oil drilling is in the Niger Delta, a swampy area near the Atlantic Ocean.

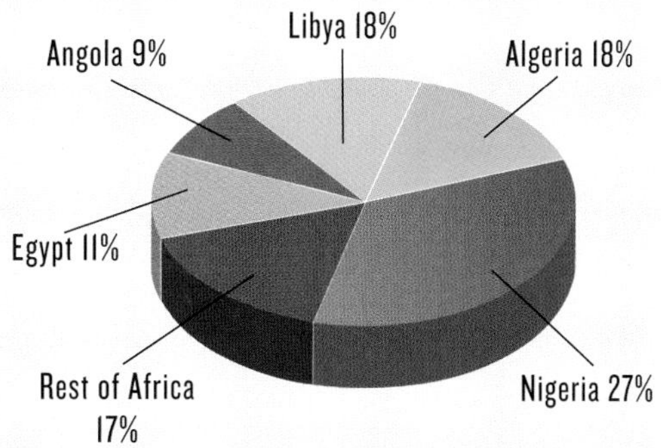

Source: Energy Information Administration

The Benefits of Oil

In some ways, oil provides great benefits for Nigeria. Money earned from oil often pays for building and improving roads and schools. It can also help pay for electricity and telephone lines for cities and towns.

Some of the international oil companies that drill in Nigeria not only pay the country to drill, but also fund programs for community development. For example, oil companies have opened job training centers for young people, and they help pay for Nigerians to attend college. One oil company built a hospital. It also set up a water ambulance to bring medical services up and down the waterways of the Niger Delta. These people might not otherwise have good health care.

Problems from Oil

With the good that oil brings to Nigeria comes the bad. The price of oil can change quickly. When the price drops, Nigeria makes less money. Projects that have been started might go unfinished. Even when prices are good, the money made from oil does not always help people who need it. Many Nigerians live in poverty.

In addition, drilling for oil can be harmful to the environment. Moving and storing oil can be dangerous and polluting. To save money, oil companies sometimes use inexpensive, less-sturdy pipes to pump oil from the ground to storage plants. These pipes sometimes break, causing oil spills that can damage the land and air.

Summing Up

Nigeria is one of the world's top oil producers. The money the country makes from oil is used to fund many useful community projects. But oil can also create problems, such as environmental damage.

South Africa After Apartheid

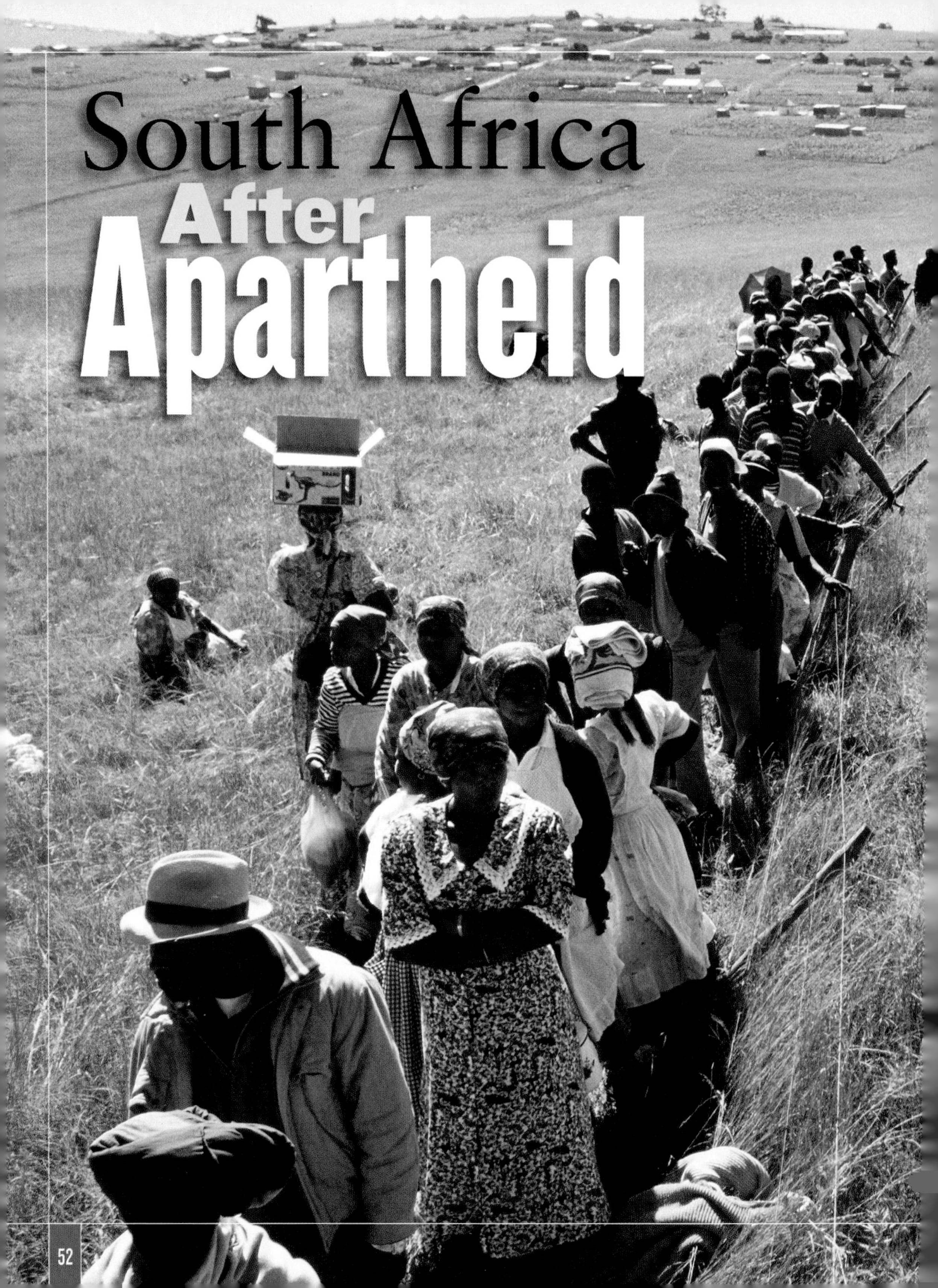

GOVERNMENT

Since 1991, the changes that have taken place in the country of South Africa have been so many and so fast that some people have called it "the miracle." For 46 years before that, South Africans had lived with a government that made different rules for different races. All that has changed. Black people, white people, Asians, and all other South Africans are now citizens with the same rights.

South Africa is a country of great diversity. In fact, it has 11 different official languages! This diversity has not always been honored by the leaders of the country. For more than 50 years, white South Africans had strict government rules called **apartheid** (uh PART eyed). Apartheid, which means "apartness" in the Afrikaans language, separated all the different groups of people.

Many black South Africans were forced to live in **homelands,** or rural areas that the government declared were not part of South Africa. Others lived in **townships**—poor, crowded areas outside of cities. Only whites were permitted to live in cities. Apartheid also let whites lead South Africa, even though there were many more black people than white people in the country. Asians and people of mixed heritages also had to follow apartheid's strict rules.

South Africans stand in a long line to vote in the country's first free election on April 27, 1994.

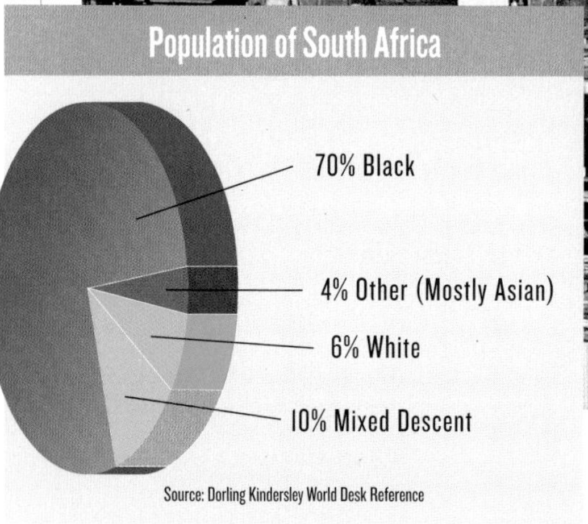

Many black South Africans still live in townships such as this one in Cape Town.

Ending Apartheid

Many South Africans fought against apartheid by speaking out and organizing protests and rallies. One leader of the struggle was a lawyer named Nelson Mandela. Because of his work against apartheid, he was arrested in 1962 and the next year was sentenced to life in prison.

By the 1980s, countries around the world were responding to the unfairness of apartheid, and they began to pressure South Africa to end it. South African athletes were not allowed to take part in international sports competitions. The United States and many other countries stopped doing as much business with South Africa because they did not want to support the apartheid government.

Under pressure from inside and outside of South Africa, laws began to change. Finally, in 1991 apartheid was ended. Nelson Mandela was released from prison.

A New Beginning

On April 27, 1994, South Africa held its first free elections, in which every South African was allowed to vote. For blacks, this meant the beginning of a government in which they could participate. The voting was scheduled to last three days. South Africans of all races waited in long lines at the polls to vote. Because so many people wanted to cast a ballot, the country had to add a fourth day to the election.

Nelson Mandela was elected the first black president of South Africa. He promised South Africans that all citizens would be treated equally.

Life After Apartheid

Under South Africa's new constitution, signed on December 10, 1996, all citizens have equal rights. The constitution pledges fair housing, health care, and schooling for all South Africans. The people and government of South Africa are working hard to make the constitution a reality.

Still, change has been slow to come in many areas of South African life. Many black South Africans still live in poverty. In the areas once set up as townships, many black South Africans still crowd together in houses made of scrap metal and cardboard. Most township residents do not have electricity or running water. In the rural areas, living conditions are similar.

Meet Ladysmith Black Mambazo

The crowd of about 100,000 people attending Mandela's inauguration ceremony were treated to many great speakers and performers. South African singing group Ladysmith Black Mambazo was one of the welcomed treats.

Joseph Shabalala began the group of 10 male singers in the 1960s. The group sings a type of music called Isicathamiya (is caht ah MEE ah), which was sung by black miners who worked far from their homes in the homelands. When they returned to the homelands, the music came with them and became a part of black South African culture and the people's struggle against apartheid.

Ladysmith Black Mambazo continues to devote itself to raising awareness about issues in South Africa and the country's musical culture. The group now plays all over the world, spreading their message of equality and peace.

Part of the problem is that there are not enough jobs. After apartheid ended, many people from other African countries came to South Africa looking for work. This means even more people began crowding South African cities like Johannesburg and Cape Town.

One way South Africa hopes to create more jobs is by attracting businesses from other countries to open branches in South Africa. More countries want to do business with South Africa, and its economy is improving. For example, since the end of apartheid, businesses from all over the world have

Since the end of apartheid, businesses from all over the world have opened new branches in South Africa, providing hundreds of new jobs.

Vanda, second from left, inspects a South African mine.

Meet Xoliswa Vanda

Although there is still much progress to be made, the end of apartheid has meant new career opportunities for some black South Africans. Deep below South Africa's surface, a gold mine is busy with the activity of 5,000 male workers—and one woman. Twenty-six-year-old Xoliswa Vanda is the first black woman ever to hold a blasting certificate in a South African gold mine. As the temperature rises above 100°F and the deafening noise of drills roars, Vanda makes important decisions about the use of explosives. "When the crews see I can do the work," she says, "that is when the men start to take me seriously. Because it is all about safety and looking out for one another."

The recent changes in South Africa have opened new opportunities, and Vanda hopes other women will follow her into the mines. As for her future, she is studying to one day become a mine manager.

Black South African students can now attend schools that were only available to white students during apartheid.

opened new branches in South Africa, providing hundreds of new jobs. South Africa is also expanding its own businesses, such as the tourism industry. Its resorts and wildlife parks attract visitors from around the world.

Education Leads the Way

Education for black South Africans may be the most improved area of life. Before apartheid, black South Africans were not allowed to attend schools with white South Africans. The schools for black South Africans had fewer books and supplies, fewer teachers, and were often very crowded. Today, all South African children can go to schools together, some in the better-equipped schools that were formerly just for white students.

Summing Up

In today's South Africa, blacks and whites are working together to strengthen the country's economy, government, and schools. There are still many challenges to be met. Many black South Africans do not have good housing, and there are not enough jobs. But education has improved, and other changes to improve the lives of all South Africans are underway.

Nelson Mandela

Nelson Mandela dedicated his life to creating a free South Africa where all people would be equal. In 1999, his political career came to an end when he stepped down from the presidency at the age of 80. Below is part of the farewell speech he made to South Africa's governing body, the Parliament.

Indeed...I have noted with deep gratitude, the generous praise that has often been given to me as an individual. But let me state this: to the extent that I have been able to achieve anything, I know that this is because I am the product of the people of South Africa.

I am the product of the rural masses who inspired in me the pride in our past and the spirit of resistance. I am the product of the workers of South Africa who, in the mines, factories, fields, and offices of our country, have pursued the principle that the interests of each are founded in the common interest of all.

I am the product of South Africa's intelligentsia [leadership], of every colour, who have laboured to give our society knowledge of itself and to fashion our people's aspirations [desires] into a realizable dream. I am the product of South Africa's business people—in industry and agriculture, commerce, and finance—whose spirit of enterprise [boldness] has helped turn our country's immense [vast] natural resources into the wealth of our nation.

To the extent that I have been able to take our country forward to this new era, it is because I am the product of the people of the world who have cherished the vision of a better life for all people everywhere. They insisted, in a spirit of self-sacrifice, that this vision should be realized in South Africa too. They gave us hope because we knew by their solidarity [unity] that our ideas could not be silenced since they were the ideas of all humanity.

Both Nelson Mandela and religious leader Desmond Tutu (left) have won Nobel Peace Prizes for their work against apartheid.

I am the product of Africa and her long-cherished dream of a rebirth that can now be realized so that all of her children may play in the sun.

When, as will be the case in a few months, I once again become an ordinary citizen of our land, it shall be as one whose concerns and capacities are shaped by the people of our land. I will count myself as among the aged of our society, as one of the rural population, as one concerned for the children and youth of our country and as a citizen of the world committed, as long as I have strength, to work for a better life for all people everywhere.

"I am the product of the people of the world who have cherished the vision of a better life for all people everywhere."

Analyzing Primary Sources

Kwame Nkrumah (to the left in white) helped Ghana win its independence in 1957.

How can you know what people thought about an event in the past as it happened? One of the best ways to find out is to read **primary sources.** These are firsthand or eyewitness accounts by people who took part in or saw an event. Letters, newspapers articles, speeches, interviews, and photographs are all examples of primary sources.

Primary sources give a sense of what an event was really like. When you read someone's letter, news account, or speech, determine the main idea and the point of view of the writer or photographer. It is important to know the point of view because the way the person feels about the event may influence what the person includes in their account.

It's time for you to analyze a primary source. First read the background information. Then read the speech. When you have finished reading, answer the questions that follow.

At long last the **battle** has **ended. . . .**

Beginning in the early 1500s, European countries ruled most African lands as colonies. In 1957 a British colony called the Gold Coast became independent. Ghana (GAH nah) would be the name of this new country. As the clock struck 12:01 a.m. on March 6, 1957, Kwame Nkrumah (KWAH may en KROO mah), Ghana's first president, made a speech in celebration of Ghana's independence. Here is an excerpt.

At long last the battle has ended. . . . And thus Ghana, your beloved country, is free forever. And here again, I want to take the opportunity to thank the chiefs, and people of this country, the youth, the farmers, the women who have so nobly fought and won this battle. . . . And as I pointed out. . . today, we must change our attitudes and our minds. We must realize that from now on, we are no more a colonial but a free and independent people. But also, as I pointed out, that entails [involves] hard work. . . .

We are going to see that we create our own African personality and identity. . . . We again rededicate ourselves in the struggle to emancipate [free] other countries in Africa; for our independence is meaningless unless it is linked up with the total liberation [freeing] of the African continent.

THINK & APPLY

- What is the main idea of the speech?
- What do you think is the mood of the speech? Give examples of Nkrumah's words to support your answer.
- What is Nkrumah's point of view about Ghana's independence? How do you know?
- Summarize the speech in your own words.

altitude height of land above sea level (p. 33)

apartheid Former South African government rules that separated different groups of people (p. 53)

biotechnology the use of science and technology to modify, or change, living things (p. 45)

Eunoto Masai ceremony celebrating the passage of young men into adulthood (p. 41)

export product sold to other countries (p. 51)

homelands in South Africa, rural areas where blacks were forced to live during apartheid (p. 53)

manyatta circle of structures built for the Masai Eunoto ceremony (p. 42)

marathon foot race over a course that is usually 26.2 miles (42 kilometers) long (p. 33)

migration movement from one place to another (p. 15)

moran a young Masai warrior (p. 41)

pull factor something that attracts a person to move to a new place (p. 18)

push factor something that causes a person to move away from a place (p. 18)

rural relating to the countryside (p. 15)

tissue culture type of biotechnology in which a section, or shoot, of one plant is used to grow more plants of the same kind (p. 46)

township in South Africa, a poor, crowded area outside of a city where many blacks lived during apartheid (p. 53)

urban relating to a city (p. 15)

urbanization the growth of cities (p. 15)

Colorful jewelery adorns young Masai women.